The Little Book of BIG Ideas: Activities Crafts & Celebrations

Terrie Sizemore

The Little Book of BIG : Activities Crafts & Celebrations
This is a work of non-fiction.

Printed in the United States of America
A 2 Z Press LLC
PO Box 582
Deleon Springs, FL 32130
bestlittleonlinebookstore.com
sizemore3630@aol.com
440-241-3126
ISBN: 978-1-954191-94-5

DEDICATION:

*To all those who are
looking for a fun idea!*

Contents

Foreword

Foreword

This little book is meant to inspire everyone. Yes, everyone. At first, I meant to create a book for adults to glean ideas for having meaningful fun with children in their lives. It didn't matter if these children were their own, grandchildren, stepchildren, Sunday school children, children of all ages being taught by adults, and more. But, as the book took shape, I wanted *everyone* to be inspired.

I spent a great deal of my adult life having fun with children. I think children make everything fun. I know how challenging it can be to try to find another great idea for a new way to have fun! I created this book as a springboard for great ideas to flow and for adults to find ways to share meaningful time with the children in their lives or adults to have meaningful times themselves.

I have learned that before you blink twice, those little ones are big ones and having little ones of their own! They need the tools and ideas to be the great adults for those young'uns as you were with them.

Not only have I had great and fun and creative times with children, I have enjoyed a lifetime of new adventures and newly creative projects. I see every day as a day to do something fun and every season as a reason to celebrate!

Unfortunately, I have witnessed others just settling in life for a mundane existence and having time just mercilessly march on and on with nothing in particular to excite them or there be something to look forward to. I hope this is not you. I believe the world is before us and all we have to do is open the curtain to find a new adventure, a new way to celebrate the same old thing, or a new creative project to embark upon!

I hope every reader enjoys this book as much as I enjoyed creating it! Every day is a great day for fun! I'm also looking forward to my next project!

A Full Year
OF FAMILY FUN
Make Memories To Last a LIFETIME With These SIMPLE Yet Super Fun Family Fun Ideas

January
- Make resolutions together
- Write out a yearly calendar Reorganize the kid's rooms
- Plan a Netflix binge day

February
- Make Love Monsters
- Build a Valentine's Day mailbox
- Make a Heart-shaped pizza
- Host a Tea Party
- Make heart shaped cookies
- Play Headbands

March
- Make or buy something green to wear
- Whip up a delicious corned beef and cabbage recipe
- Celebrate St. Patrick's Day
- Play Uno
- Go on a coffee date
- Make a Spring bucket list

April
- Host an Egg hunt
- Take a drawing class
- Go to a museum
- Play outside
- Make an Easter dessert
- Play Easter bingo

May
- Breakfast in Bed for Mom is always a good idea
- Go for a drive with the windows down
- Have a dance party
- Make a Summer bucket list
- Head to a baseball game

June
- Host an outdoor movie night
- Create sun catchers for your windows
- Build a birdhouse
- Read books about Summer, the beach and animals found in the water

July
- Host a 4th of July BBQ
- Find the best red, white and blue traditions
- Create a patriotic playlist
- Set up a make your own sundae bar

August
- Make a fun back to school craft
- Play Monopoly
- Read all your favorite back to school classics

September
- Make a delicious apple crumble
- Celebrate Grandparents day
- Head to your local Fall festival
- Make a fun fall-themed craft

October
- Paint Your Pumpkin
- Carve A Jack 'O Lantern
- Make A Pumpkin Flavored Treat
- Host A Halloween Themed Brunch
- Play A Halloween Themed Game

November
- Crunch through the leaves
- Let the kids make something for Thanksgiving
- Make a fun turkey-themed treat for their class
- Read books about Thanksgiving

December
- Wrap gifts
- Feed a reindeer
- Take pictures with Santa
- Read a Christmas story before bed every night
- Write a letter to SantaGo caroling
- Watch your favorite Christmas movies
- Make a playlist of your favorite holiday tunes

Why Activities, Crafts, & Celebrations?

Important For Everyone

I'm a kid at heart. I think being young at heart is the secret to staying young — thinking and acting young! It thrills me to consider a new craft project, find new ways to celebrate the same old holidays, or make some plans — even if those plans are just to have lunch with a friend.

Crafting, celebrating holidays, and doing different and interesting things not only make our lives happy and enriched, they are fun. I am convinced there is always something to look forward to when we see the days of our lives worth celebrating and doing new and fun things to provide us with pleasure and satisfying activities.

I watched people I love systematically withdraw from any fun activities. Things that were once exciting to them were no longer exciting. Once they loved going to the beach until, one day, they no longer did. There was a time we walked a path at a nearby refuge, went to local springs to kayak or search for manatees, bike ride, and more. My loved ones said they didn't want to do these things any longer. These things no longer held any interest to them.

It hurts my heart to say I told one loved one she needed to find *something* that continued to make her happy. And, whatever that *something* was, I would be glad to enjoy it with her. One of her journal entries said, 'August 1, 2021 — These past days have been television or the phone. Nothing really fun. Oh, I enjoy talking to my sister, but I wish when I got to bed, I'd feel satisfied - like I used to – but all feels empty and wasted and my life is flying by.'

I want to inspire every reader to believe life can be wonderful each and every day and provide ideas and inspiration to have fun – or ideas to inspire 'other' ideas. I realize age brings challenges that make it difficult to continue to have happy days or do things we once may have been able to, but I believe we must try. I believe studies confirm that enjoying life is good for our mental health and our general well-being. There is always something to enjoy.

Important For Adults

Research and personal experience have confirmed that crafting and fun activities, as well as celebrating, bolster our mood, improve our self-confidence and self-esteem, reduce stress, sometimes improve our overall health, and are just plain fun and great activities any time. Having something to look forward to makes life enjoyable.

The Bible tells us that God has special things for each season of our lives. (Psalms 103.5 Amplified) He is never at a loss for how to make our lives enriched and wonderful. I believe the God Who created all we see and enjoy wants us to enjoy what He has so lavishly provided for us to enjoy.

I don't think we need special talents to enjoy life, just a 'want to' to enjoy it and a willingness to try different things. There are many more activities, crafts, and ways to celebrate than I could ever cover in this little book, but here goes with my ideas!

Important For All Children

Crafting, celebrating, and doing new and fun activities are especially important to children. There are so many benefits to helping children develop emotionally and mentally as well as they develop their technical skills while completing craft projects and activities to celebrate holidays.

New and fun activities also provide treasured memories children can carry throughout their lives. Life is difficult for many but we can make the very most of each day to help the difficult moments seem easier.

Many children face the challenge of blended families or lost parents or even disabilities. These children need activities that help them grow despite the struggles they face.

Some activities are also educational. Children love to have fun and there are many ways to make learning fun without them even *knowing* that they are learning! So many activities double as fun projects and projects to use to learn.

Crafts can be a tool to help the development and growth of our children in a fun way. These pictures are precious because they show us how both adults and children have so much fun doing projects together. FYI - It seems children are able to use scissors by the time they are four years old. I help the younger ones more so.

Crafts are also a fun way to show love and approval and build self-esteem in little ones. It doesn't really seem to matter what craft or activity we choose; children seem to love everything and they make everything fun.

For young children, I feel crafting is extremely instrumental in developing and improving gross and fine motor skills – even if it looks like scribble. Every child benefits from art and fun projects.

4

There are so many fun things to choose from. Glittering – glitter application as is seen here is always a great project for coordination skills. In addition, cutting paper as we saw before, combining different types of papers, painting, coloring with markers or crayons, and more all help the developing child. And, did I mention, it's fun!

Children learn reading and speaking skills as they read instructions and interact with adults and other children to complete cooking or crafting projects.

They also learn to follow directions during certain activities that can provide memory skills as well. Adults can ask the child why they 'chose a certain color' or other interactive questions as they 'play' and engage with their child. This helps adults evaluate how their child is enjoying and understanding the activity they are doing. It also provides an opportunity to share the adult's experiences with the child.

5

I always enjoyed doing various crafts, celebratory activities, or other activities with my stepdaughter. It was an opportunity for me to enjoy a younger time in my life all over again!

While participating in crafting or other activities, children also develop good and needed eye-hand coordination, measuring skills, learn simple math and spatial concepts such as shapes, and even problem solve.

Spending time with adults and completing projects also builds self-esteem and encourages a child's creativity. Crafts promote thinking, exploring, discovering, problem-solving, and imagining new things and improve school work.

Spending this time together also promotes a feeling of bonding with the adults crafting with them or doing many celebrating activities and/or other activities, and more.

I have come to realize that children may not know how to express their feelings about many things, but I am certain they treasure the chance to spend time with the adults in their lives, and what better way than crafting or some fun activity?

Children can create something they can have for years and remember the time they spent doing this. These types of memories make children feel worthy of love and attention when they receive it in positive ways as a child spending time with adults who encourage them and make much over them. This makes them want to try new things.

Children feel they are BIG and accomplished something wonderful. Make much of these little ones, they need it! I remember the sweet look on my stepdaughter's face and the other children's faces when I looked them in their eyes and said, 'You did a good job!' I smile as I think of their little faces. They like seeing they can improve too.

Adults can spend time talking with their children as well as work together on the project. I believe that children desperately need to get away from those electronic screens anyway and do something real with their little hands.

In addition, there are times we adults need to find ways to educate and help our children along without a sign that says – LESSON TIME. On the other hand, maybe lesson time isn't such a bad idea, but one has to know their child.

Sometimes children resist 'forced education,' but love to work on a creative project or do some activity that could be very educational.

For instance, I recently learned that Boxing Day originated in Britain and was celebrated the day after Christmas when the alms box, which were collection boxes for the poor and kept mostly in the church, were opened and distributed to children. This is a great activity to show children how to be kind and giving. Be sneaky and teach children many things!

There are many different holidays or customs around the world and at home the children can have a blast learning about. Pick a new celebration to learn about today!

I try to always remember, they're not 'just clay' candy dishes those children make for their moms on Mother's Day, they are loving gifts from the heart that parents treasure for a lifetime and show the children how special they truly are to their loving parents.

Nothing says, 'I love you,' like a little something from our little ones!

It's not just a ride in the country on Sunday. It's time spent talking and laughing and playing car games about spotting different things around them; memories children carry with them forever.

It's about having fun with the little ones in our lives or other adults and sometimes just ourselves.

My aim in this book is to help when we ask, 'Just what can we do to make childhood special, bond with our children, and help them know how much they are loved?' or 'Just what can I do for fun today?' And do it!!!!

Sometimes I'm stumped and my life seems to be going at a speed of ninety miles per hour but I need to throttle it back and make some great new memories.

9

I want to explore the different ideas I have to share in the chapters to follow. I believe what we do matters to not only help our children grow into well-adjusted and happy adults, it helps them see God as a loving and dependable Father as well. I believe the hearts of our children are in our hands and the most important thing they want from us is our love. Spending time with our children, as well as doing fun things with them, are, in my opinion, the most important things we can do to demonstrate our love for them and allow them to know our love.

It all sounds daunting at times, but it isn't really. Children are simple, resilient, and very, very, very, very forgiving if we don't do everything perfectly. They are only small for a short time but can be children at heart always.

EXHILARATE : to make someone very happy and excited or elated! I don't think we necessarily have to run head-first down a raging river, but we can find some pretty awesome things to do in this little book.

My Experience

I have always been a creative person and love the creative process. I watch talented crafters turn vines into beautiful wreaths and others who do spectacular things with lace or small pieces of glass or metal – like using sea glass to create a lovely Christmas tree. I admit I don't have the same talent as some, but I still love to participate in any craft I have the supplies and ability for.

Celebrating is something else I enjoy. Like many others, Christmas is one of my favorite times of the year to celebrate. It makes me happy to decorate and I feel it makes the season more meaningful if I am more engaged.

I feel fun activities, celebrating holidays and special occasions, and crafting are also meaningful for young children. I have great memories of all the different things I made throughout the years and the time I spent making them. Also, I have collected many, many photo albums that remind me of happy moments with those I love.

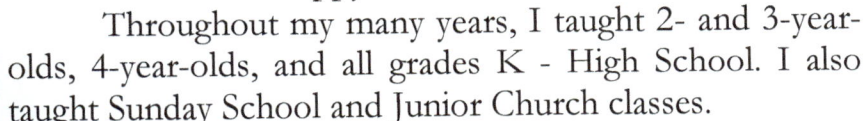

Throughout my many years, I taught 2- and 3-year-olds, 4-year-olds, and all grades K - High School. I also taught Sunday School and Junior Church classes.

For most lessons and day activities, I developed a craft to help the children remember the lesson and have fun creating something they could be proud of. Even if it was just a rainbow to remember Noah and his ark, the children enjoyed our time together.

In addition, I have many interests and am grateful for this. I enjoy horseback riding, kayaking, bike riding, walking, shopping, gardening, painting, working with clay, playing piano, violin, guitar, and more.

There aren't enough hours in the day to do all the fun things I would love to do. I enjoyed time spent with my disabled brother-in-law when we visited a local rose garden, had lunch together, and other things. My sister and I share a love for shopping and the beach. Life feels full and satisfying to me when I have something to look forward to and can do something that makes a new memory for me. I have little problem finding something fun to do!

So, let's get started on all the ideas I want to share with you to help you have some fun today!

2

Supplies

Various Craft Items That
Will Come in Handy

Everyone needs tools. Tools for crafting and fun activities and celebrating may be more specific in the pages to come, but I want to address some in general here.

Many craft supplies are inexpensive. They range from simple, household items to expensive tools/supplies that can be used for many projects.

I have several totes with my various supplies but must admit I lose track of many things and no matter how organized I think I am. I still find myself wondering where I put all my different supplies.

Shopping can be fun and there are many stores with the things you need.

Coloring Books – Always fun for the young ones. There are adult coloring books as well that some find relaxing and enjoyable. Children have been enjoying coloring books for years. They are usually their first introduction into the world of art.

Colored construction paper or card stock paper – this can be used for many art or craft projects, comes in all colors, and number of pages that can be purchased.

Craft paint – the type depends on age. Paint can make with whip cream and food color for safe paint for very young children. We may also choose watercolor, finger paint, acrylics, paint for sun catchers, paint pencils, or oils for older children.

Paint brushes – all different sizes

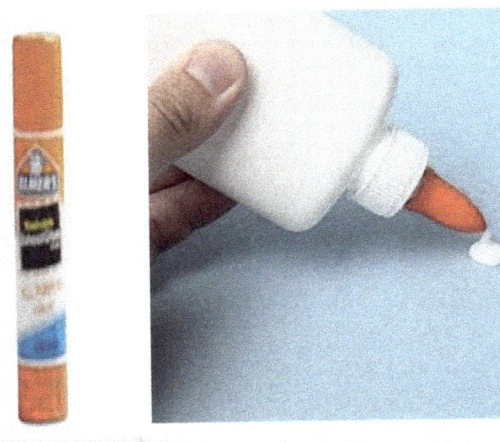

Glue – comes in stick or liquid white glue. Glue sticks work well for very young children due to being less messy but can be used for all ages. White glue is great for older children and adults with more developed skills.

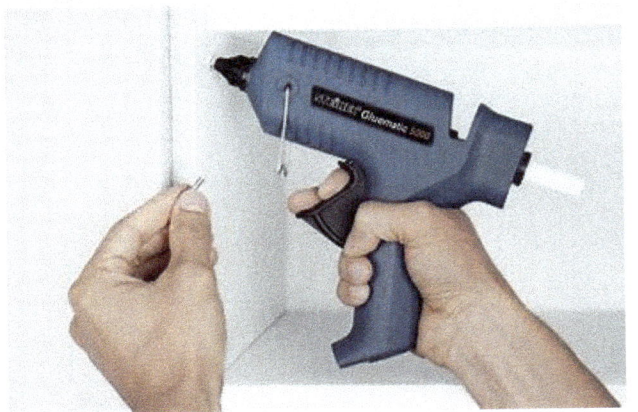

Glue guns – are super easy and convenient to use, but should always be used with an adult.

15

Scissors – I pick blunt child scissors for young children. It is my experience that children don't do scissor activity well until they are about four years old. Some may disagree and have some talented younger children who handle scissor activity just fine. But please consider thinking about close supervision with scissors as the best idea. Always be safe.

Paper plates / cups / Styrofoam / environment – some environmentally conscious adults and children may want to avoid Styrofoam products but cups and balls can be used in many crafts or art projects.

Pom poms –are fun for projects

16

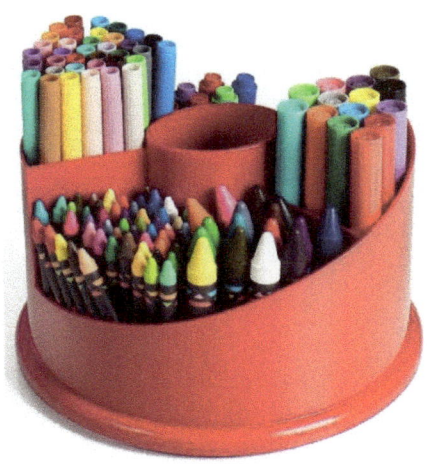

Markers and crayons – are good to have many of these handy with many colors and these are not expensive.

Chalk – is always fun on driveways, sidewalks, and indoor chalkboards

Googly eyes – of different sizes

Tissue paper

Glitter – different colors

Pipe cleaners

Feathers

Popsicle sticks – many cute
projects can be created
from popsicle sticks

18

Balloons – for fun or
water balloon fun

Plaster/paper animals to paint

Stamps

19

Clothes pins

Sponges

Smooth rocks – of various shapes and sizes

Yarn and needles and hooks – for so many fun projects!

3

Let's Get Crafting

It should be obvious I love colorful things! Yes, there are reportedly ten million colors in the world and I think we should enjoy all of them!

Painting – watercolor is my personal favorite, but I recommend selecting safe paints that are not toxic to children. Children love finger painting, brush painting on canvas, wood, plastic, heavy paper, and more. Non-toxic paints are available. Small children can enjoy finger painting items with paint made by cleverly using whipping cream with added food coloring. It's edible!

Painting allows eye-hand skill development, is easy to do, and makes projects colorful. I picked some pictures to show that art doesn't have to be perfect to be something special.

Gluing and cutting – there are so many projects with cutting and gluing skills. Children can cut pictures from magazines or use family photos to make a collage. Also, they can create cute pictures that use their imagination like this one.

One of my favorite cut-and-glue crafts is making the animals for Noah's ark, the ark itself, and gluing all the parts together.

Drawing – I encourage children to draw. Some are excellent artists and some need help. A friend recommended drawing something every day. He said this makes it easier to master the art of art. TIP: Try to avoid the wall if possible.

Shadow boxes – are a cute way to create a story as well as make something beautiful. Sometimes children are asked to do shadowboxes for stories at school. I made one for the State of Florida and all the fun I've had here.

Clay – some just use clay to mold a vase or cup or candy dish and some are skilled enough to use a pottery wheel.

Making candles – There are kits to make candles and some recipes are available as well.

22

Beads – are a great, fun way to create wearable jewelry. There are kits to bead. Young children and older children enjoy this craft.

Origami – usually I suggest this for older children because it can be very complicated. There are basic, easy origami projects for young children that may be challenging.

Fun photography – taking pictures is an art children can learn at any time. Nature and pictures of family or friends can be pretty darn fun!

Chalk drawing – can be as simple as a rainbow on the sidewalk to a fun chalkboard in the house to leave messages on or creating a picture for a happy day to very detailed chalk art.

23

No matter what
you choose,

Whether it's paper plates into dinos or other animals…….

Or making a globe covered in stamps…

Making animals from paper….

Homemade stamps or homemade cards…..

25

Find fun uses for feathers and popsicle sticks.....

Or discover even more paper animals

26

Or find even more fun things to do with clay, buttons, and more popsicle sticks....

It's easy to see that crafts are fun, great for everyone of all ages, help show love for each other, create fun news things and are altogether wonderful!

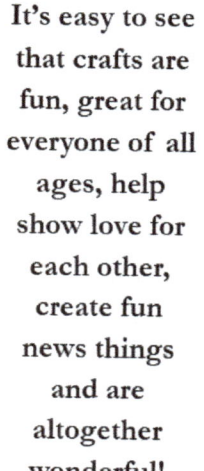

39 Easy Craft Projects For Adults

So, get together with friends or a group or just by yourself is okay and get ready to have some fun!

DIY FUN

There's just
so much
you can do!

And when you're all finished, get ready to show us your best stuff!!!

In Conclusion

I think it's safe to say that there is *always* a fun craft you can do to create something new or have a wonderfully enjoyable time with your child or friends or yourself. The internet and library are filled with ideas. Also, ETSY and other sites have craft corners with cute ideas. We'll explore some crafting ideas as well as celebrating ideas and activities in the next sections of these books. Activity is the A word here. So, grab some supplies and get to work! And did I mention - don't forget to have fun!

4

Christmas Crafts and Activities

There are way too many crafts and activities to include them all in one book, however, I want to do my best to show just how fun Christmas is!

My first Christmas activity to mention is candlelight Christmas Eve service at a local church. It has always been one of my favorite times and I have precious memories of attending service one Christmas Eve before my brother went to heaven. It was nice to see him and my family in church together singing carols and worship songs.

Since Jesus is the Reason for the Season, I like to include this as we get busy with holiday preparations, gifts, and the food we enjoy at this time of year.

Christmas is truly my favorite time of year. Not only Christmas, though, but all holidays and special celebrations like birthdays and anniversaries.

I don't know a great deal about Hanukah, but I think anyone reading this book can guess I find *any* reason to celebrate is a great reason to celebrate, so Hanukah sounds like something really fun to celebrate and learn about as well as the Christmas holiday. I found some fun crafts and activities for Hanukah I will share in the next chapter.

Decorating

Back to Christmas! Decorating can be something that puts everyone in the holiday spirit. There was a time I had four Christmas trees – all decorated to the max – and a Christmas village, outside lights, and more. I enjoyed putting up all the decorations with my stepdaughter and we had laughs and talk time while doing it. The only downside was putting it all away after the holidays.

Some don't want to do the 'work' it takes to decorate elaborately, but any decoration is something. My sister has a 'Charlie Brown' tree that sits on her kitchen table. This is all my sister has for holiday decorations at her home.

It's been many years since I put up elaborate decorations. Not having my own home and needing to care for family members has limited my ability to celebrate, but to enjoy Christmas all the time, I decided to keep my Christmas decorations on display all year round. I know I'm not alone on this, but the trouble for me is that I have so many decorations I'm sure it looks odd to some to see them up when they visit in May. I just say, 'It will be Christmas in July soon!'

So, what's on your list of homemade craft decorations? They are so much fun too. From popsicle stick crafts …

Ornaments for the tree,

stringing popcorn, or other festive things for garland, and making pine roping decorations with red bows have always been favorites for me.

Decorating little trees to set around the house is another great craft for the little ones.

Activities for Celebrating

There are so many activities, they could fill many books. I want to share a few of my favorite things to do at Christmas time and am sure you have many traditions you may want to share. Sometimes one idea shared leads to another and enriches my list of good times. I hope this is true for you.

Thankful ABCs

ABCs can be used for encouraging a thankful heart in a child as well as anyone. I get my list out and start writing and thanking God for all He has given to me in my life and every holiday season.

A – is for angels, antlers of the reindeer, the Advent and Advent calendars I love so much, appreciation for the blessings, the aroma of all the treats and fragrances of Christmas like cinnamon, and others.

B – if for Baby Jesus, belief, beauty, Bethlehem, Bible, boots, bows, busy, baking cookies and cakes, bells I love to hear, blessings I have each day – like food, clothes, and more, and we mustn't forget Santa's beard.

C – Christmas, cake, candles, chimney, candy, carols, celebrate, charity, cookies, chocolate.

D – decorations, Dear Santa, Dancer, Dasher, dinner, desserts, and more!

And so on – to XYZ – eXciting, X's and O's, xylophone for Christmas, yuletide, yule log, yam, YEAH, yummy/yummylicious, yellow, youngsters, zazzy, zest and everything our imaginations can dream and think of.

And you can think of MORE – a great time of year to be thankful and always finding ways to do so makes it fun too.

Gingerbread Houses

Gingerbread houses. Everyone can make a cute little house! My stepdaughter and I used kits or the library had activities to make them. Sometimes recreation centers or schools have a time they invite children and families to make gingerbread houses.

Homemade Christmas Cards

Homemade cards are always a big hit with children and adults. They can utilize all the skills mentioned in the craft section of this book as well as their holiday imagination. The cards can be for the elderly in nursing homes or children in hospitals or for friends and family.

Baking

Baking is a great way to involve children of all ages. They can help measure, mix, roll dough, and taste test all the goods. Great family fun.

And baking can help children or adults make edible gifts like these:

Additional homemade gifts can be jars with candy or hot cocoa or soup ingredients. Jars stuffed with pine cones or eucalyptus are fun as well.

Pies, cookies, treats like peppermint bark, cupcakes, and more are splendidly fun during the holidays and can be shared with family, friends, taken to church class, school class, nursing homes, or shared with others like the homeless or shut-ins.

Cookie Swaps or Just for You and Your Family

Speaking of cookies above, a cookie swap is a great way to share with friends or other family members and sample different cookies each year.

Decorating the cookies is a great activity for young children as well as being able to sample their work!

Some people are great bakers and have their own special holiday cookies. Since I don't have a 'white' thumb, I call it, for baking unique treats, I rely on others to contribute those cookies and I am assigned chocolate chip or oatmeal raisin cookies!

Holiday Crafts

In addition to the popsicle stick ornaments and garland and gingerbread houses, and homemade cards above, there are so many crafts a child or adult can enjoy creating for the holiday season that they cannot all be represented here, but a few of them are included here and there are many more! All a few of my favorite things!

Ornaments can be made one year and saved for years to come. I have a collection of my own.

Christmas trees can be painted, made with popsicle sticks, felt pieces, and MORE. This tree on the left is really cute and BIG with things to put on it – reindeer, candy canes, balls, snowmen, sweet gingerbread kids, bells, presents, and more!

40

Just like Christmas trees
can come in all shapes
and sizes and crafts....

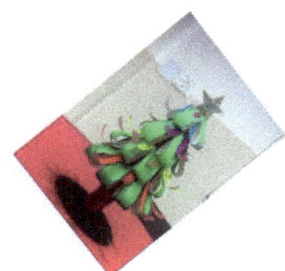

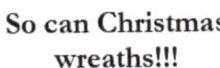

So can Christmas
wreaths!!!

Toy Drive

Toy drives are wonderful ways to encourage benevolence in children. The entire Christmas season is about sharing and caring. What better way to do so than to make sure every child has a toy to open on Christmas – maybe more than one!

Soup Kitchen – Feed the Homeless and Hungry

Ministries that help the less fortunate are also a way of helping children develop a benevolent spirit. I feel this is the heart of Jesus. He said, 'Whatever you do to the least of these, you do to Me,' and 'If you give a cup of cold water in the Name of Jesus, you will never lose your reward.' Love the motto – Serve like you are serving a King!

Visit Widows / Shut-Ins / Orphanages /Hospitals

There truly are so many that are lonely and, even though we cannot visit everyone, we can visit someone. Each family knows a widow or shut-in. Orphanages are filled with those who may feel forgotten at holiday or other times.

It's a lovely gesture to organize a visit with your family or a group of friends or a small church group and give a basket of small personal items such as soaps, wipes, lotions, or cookies and treats. Sometimes cards are nice with small gift cards for a nearby coffee shop. Calling ahead and seeing what may bless others helps decide what to do as well.

Advent Calendars

I have always loved Advent calendars. Each year I look forward to having my calendar by December 1st and then counting down 25 days until Christmas. If you are really industrious, you can make your own. I usually purchase one. There are all sorts.

Advent calendars range from Christmas trees with small boxes so a treat can be found behind each door to a peg board you or your little one can hang a small ornament on each peg to celebrate the holiday. Some can have little messages with things to do each day and some have ornaments that stick to the tree to decorate it more and more each day. Some are simple little bags with fun treats for each day

of the advent. I even spotted one of a string of buckets. We have to use our great imaginations to decide what to do with these. They are cute and perhaps could have a small toy or treat inside!

Caroling

Caroling is always another holiday favorite activity.

Elf on the Shelf or other 'in crowd' New Trends

My cousin and her children love to have Elf on the shelf at their home. Laura puts him around the house and the boys find him in all the fun places.

Library Activities or Church or Rec Centers

Be on the lookout for holiday activities anywhere you can join. Some are free and that was always my favorite price while we were raising our young family.

Sled riding if you have snow

Sled riding was one of my favorite things to do. Now that I live where our chance of snow each day in winter is 0% - ha ha – we do not sled ride. But if you live where the white fluff falls, have a ball!! I have fond memories of packing our sleds, winter wear, and a thermos filled with hot cocoa and heading for the tallest and most snow-filled hills we could find each snow season. It was always greatest when it first snowed that year. It's a great activity for families to do together and for Christmas time too.

Watch the Nutcracker

I love ballet. Some may be saying they'd rather do anything in the entire world than watch ballet, but I think it's great to give children the opportunity to enjoy something cultural. The music is tremendous and the dancing superb! It's a holiday classic and boys may like it as much as girls. In fact, those boys will be boyfriends and husbands one day, and perhaps it will enhance their romantic endeavors to know about such a wonderfully beautiful ballet.

Holiday Movies

Each year I look forward to all the classics – 'It's a Wonderful Life,' 'A Christmas Carol,' 'Rudolph the Red-Nosed Reindeer,' and more.

I also have to admit I write down all the new holiday movies the various channels have created for our viewing pleasure each year. The lists keep growing and growing each year. I wonder what will be new this year?

Christmas Word Scramble for kids

A fun game for the little ones.

Drive and Look at Lights

Another great holiday favorite for the family to enjoy. Some families really go all out to decorate each year.

Build a Christmas Village

A very creative way to make a holiday favorite activity.

Christmas Around the World

We learned about Boxing Day earlier. Children enjoy learning about Christmas around the world in other places too. For instance, did you know that in England families leave mince pies for Santa instead of cookies and milk? And Italy was where the first nativity was displayed and on January 5th, excited children in Italy prepare for a late-night visit from La Befana by hanging up socks that will be filled with small delights. Befana is a grandmotherly woman who resembles a kindly witch. She brings gifts to the good children by depositing them in the stockings hung about the hearth then she tidies up with her broom before she leaves.

There are so many fun facts for children to learn about Christmas in different countries. Pick a new one each year!

Read Favorite Holiday Books

Reading holiday books is a special tradition for many families during the Christmas season. Read old and new books and make it a tradition in your home!

Take a Sleigh Ride

If you're lucky and live with snow and horses, this is very fun! And this is not all!

5

Hanukkah Crafts and Activities

Everyone can celebrate holidays. This chapter briefly shares some ideas for a fun and exciting Hanukkah holiday celebration.

DIY Maccabee Cookie Boxes  Hanukkah-shaped cookie cutters

Jewish Holiday Cookie Box

Hanukkah Cookie Mix in a Jar

  Hanukkah crackers or potato chips

The Star of David

I'm convinced there are more uses for celebrating with the beloved Star of David than I could possibly cover here, but here are a few sweet activities to consider! Even Christians would enjoy these crafts.

Star of David cupcake toppers or

Hanukkah cupcake craft – using different shades of blue frosting and placed in the shape of the Star of David.

Foil tape serving tray – made with the Star of David

Star of David window stars

Star of David Place Settings
– made with sticks with leaves

Star of David eucalyptus craft
with wood and added decorations

And, while working on the Star of David
crafts, you can whip us some cupcakes
with Hanukkah sprinkles

Or make a marshmallow dreidel
Hanukkah Craft – with Hebrew on them

Dreidels with glitter

Other Dreidel Crafts Include:

Hanging dreidels

Paper dreidels

Menorah Crafts

There are probably many
ways children and families can enjoy
making menorahs. This one is a
paper flower menorah ......

This is another one made of flowers......

This one is a wood block menorah....

And, last, but not least of my samples, my
favorite, a candy menorah craft for kids!

51

Candle Crafts

Floating Blue tea lights

DIY Crayon Candles or stacked Candles

And another great idea for
Hanukkah is a songbook !

There are many more crafts to consider every season!

6

Easter Crafts and Activities

As a woman of faith, Easter is the most significant celebration of all. Since the remembrance is about our Risen Savior, I make sure I have fun during the season, but remember the true meaning as well.

Since I am a veterinarian and have raised chicks, I find some of the Easter crafts more darling than the next! Not only the chicks, the bunny lollipops are very cute too!

Egg maracas are a cute craft for the children to shake while singing Easter songs.

There are many ways to craft the **empty tomb** and the Risen Savior. Cute crafts for the children!

Crosses for bookmarks are a favorite Easter
craft. Some can be colored by the children and some can
be made specially as a thoughtful gift.

Since I'm a painter, I love thumbprint crosses
that are a colorful reminder
of our Savior's loving sacrifice for
His children on the Cross.

Cross necklaces help young
ones remember our Savior
on the Cross and what
Jesus did for them.

Easter wreaths are always fun!

Baskets for poor children – filled with stuffed animals, candy, little books about Jesus, and more are a great way to help children share.

Easter egg coloring and crafts are also great fun

EASTER BIBLE QUIZ

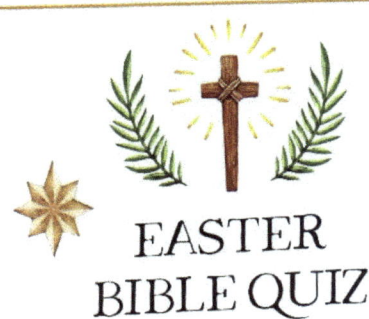

EASTER BIBLE QUIZ

1. What does Palm Sunday mark?

2. Why is the Sunday before the resurrection called Palm Sunday?

3. Why was Jesus coming to Jerusalem?

4. When Jesus entered Jerusalem during what is known as His Triumphal Entry, what animal was He riding on?

5. On what day was the Last Supper had?

6. How did Judas betray Jesus?

7. Where did the arrest of Jesus take place?

8. Who was Pontius Pilate?

9. Who was the criminal who was set free so that Jesus could be crucified?

10. Who else was crucified alongside Jesus?

11. What words did Jesus, according to the Bible, cry out while on the cross?

13. Which disciple cut off the ear of the high priest's servant in an attempt to protect Jesus from being taken as a prisoner?

14. How many times did Peter deny Christ after the abandoned the Lord?

15. How many pieces of silver did Judas trade the life of Jesus for?

16. What did Pilate's wife counsel him to do concerning Jesus?

17. Jesus was crucified at Calvary also known as Golgotha, what do these words mean in Hebrew?

18. A man named Simon was compelled to carry the cross of Jesus. In Mark 15 we are told the names of Simon's two sons. What were their names?

19. What kind of crown was placed upon Jesus' head?

20. The bible states that Jesus was scourged. What does the word scourge mean?

21. "Take ye him, and crucify him, for I find no fault in him.". Who made this statement?

22. In repentance Judas returned the money to the priests that he was given as the price of betrayal of the Lord and then did what?

23. When Jesus died there was darkness in the land. How long did it last?

24. In John 19 two men helped prepare the body of Christ for burial. One is said to have been a secret disciple and another secretly came to Jesus early in His ministry to ask question. Who were these men?

25. How many gospels are in the bible?

26. What kind of cloth was used to wrap the body of Jesus?

27. How many angels, according to the Gospel of John, were inside the sepulchre?

28. After being resurrected, Jesus shows himself to the disciples beside which sea?

PRINT GO GO

Games of all Sorts are Great Fun

And Don't Forget the Baking

You can try some bunny tails......

....bunny pancakes.…...

.…...cookies decorated.…..

….. or crunchy mix.…..

are some great ideas for Easter!

7

Passover Crafts and Activities

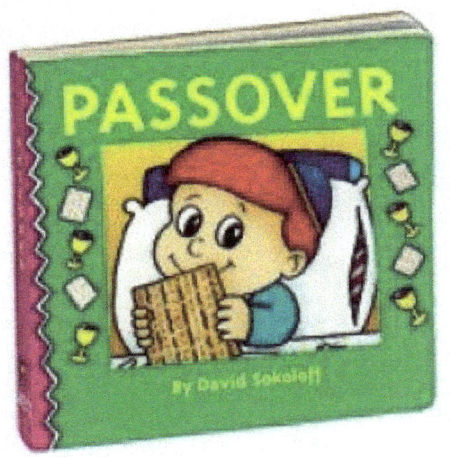

For young children of all faiths, there are cute books to share the meaning of Passover.

Seder plates made from paper plates are cute crafts.

60 CARDS + PACKAGE BOX

PASSOVER MEMORY GAME

Bible Quiz
Passover (Pesach)

Match the question with the answer on the right.

_____ How many plagues did Yah send on Egypt?

_____ How did the Israelites protect themselves from the final plague?

_____ What did the Israelites take with them when they left Egypt?

_____ When does the Passover take place?

_____ What food does the Bible say to eat at Passover?

_____ Yeshua was from which tribe of Israel?

_____ Where was Yeshua crucified?

_____ At which festival did 12-year-old Yeshua stay behind at the Temple?

_____ What was happening at the Temple while Yeshua hung on the cross?

_____ Who owned the tomb where Yeshua was placed?

1. Lamb, bread, and bitter herbs (Exo 12)
2. Unleavened bread
3. Passover
4. Ten
5. Judah
6. Unblemished lambs were being killed
7. Joseph of Arimathea
8. Golgotha
9. Painted lamb's blood on their door-posts
10. At twilight on the 14th day of Aviv (March/April)

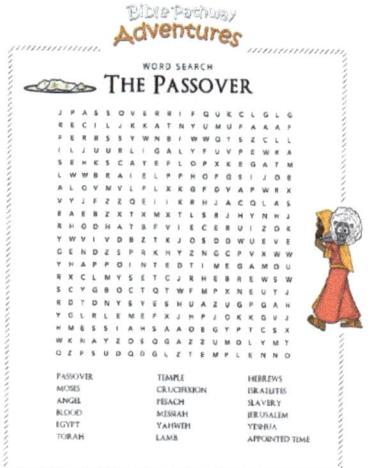

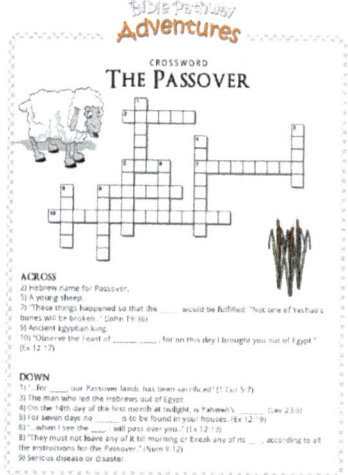

There are many different games to play during Passover.

And Don't Forget the Baking

Matzo ball soup

Cheese Latkes

Mushroom, Harissa, and
Goat Cheese Frittata

Kid's favorite pizza

Passover cobbler

Matzo Huevos Rancheros

and barbecue chicken latkes sliders

are just a few of the delicious food
ideas for celebrating Passover

8

Birthday Crafts and Activities

Everyone loves a party! Get all your friends and friends of friends
and family and everyone you can think of together and have a blast! My
family loves to celebrate. We celebrate on the beach, in the park,
at a spaghetti dinner, a favorite restaurant, a nursing home
where one of our loved ones lived, many more places,
and, last but not least, home.
Presents may be a good idea for children and many adults, but not
always mandatory. Just a great celebration makes any occasion happy.

And, did I mention – DON'T forget the cake!

9

Cooking With Children, Friends, or for Yourself

The truth is I'm not a great cook. I get by, but it's a challenge for me. But I so love food. I have friends who are great cooks and I've always enjoyed being invited for a meal. My mom and sister are also really good cooks and both my grandmothers were good cooks as well as my aunt. I think I included them all – ha ha.

Once, when I was a little girl, lost at the dinner table with many family members, one of my grandmothers served homemade chicken and dumplings. They were so good I remember thinking to myself, 'I would love more of that.'

One other time, I cooked a shrimp recipe for my mother and she had a second helping! I think that was the biggest compliment anyone ever gave me about a meal because I had a reputation for not being able to do more than boil water.

In some seasons of my life, I've made it a goal – or personal challenge - to try a new recipe every week. I have many cookbooks at home, ask others for recipes if I enjoyed something they made, or I visit the library for books to seek out recipes. I have even 'googled' different things for something new to try to cook.

I hate to admit that 'easy to follow' recipes are best for me. I don't do complicated meals like my sister and one of my friends are, what I consider, brave enough to try. You can choose what works for you and your friends or children. I love chicken cordon-blue, chicken paprikash, and beef stroganoff – since I'm not vegetarian – but these are a bit more advanced than my skill level. If you are vegetarian, vegetable lasagna is great as well.

I'm not sure how some become great cooks or bakers, but one friend said her mom was an excellent cook and taught her. That made her a great cook as well. She just knew how to put things together and season them well.

Reading Recipes

I remember another time watching a good friend show her daughter how to make meatloaf. As I watched her teach her daughter, I was envious because I never had a cooking lesson at my home. It seems to me this is how some become good cooks. But, to be honest, some just come to the skill naturally.

I think cooking and baking are great ways to bond with children as well as teach them how to cook and bake as well as learn other skills like measuring and such. Children love helping and they love learning, especially when they don't even realize they *are* learning!

So, no matter what you want to bake or cook, whether you choose hamburgers or mac and cheese, cookies for a holiday, just for fun, or a bake sale at school or church, or something new with chicken or such, dress up your little chef and get to work!

You can both whip up a batch of your favorite cookies or cupcakes and have your child measure items, mix and spoon out dough or pour dough into proper baking ware, and time the baking to make sure everything is done. They can learn about hot safety and using mitts or pot holders to avoid injuries.

Measuring and Rolling

Young men make great chefs. Sometimes it's a challenge to find things to do with boys and dads, but there are many ways they can cook together. Reading instructions and following instructions as well as measuring are all skills the young ones can learn and benefit by.

Young men are not only cute as they rise to the challenges of baking and cornbread muffins, they also are very serious about things and do a great job when given the opportunity.

I enjoy working with young men because they stick with the tasks we set out to accomplish and I see the pride in their eyes when they do a good job. My girlfriend's two boys are this way.

Who doesn't love making memories with Grandma? Or mom too?

Bonding

Spending time with our little ones is priceless to me. They are always happy to spend time. Everything in life shows us how happy they are.

They can have a sense of accomplishment as well as create something healthy for themselves and learn something that will last a lifetime.

We talked about self-esteem and some children need a little more help than others, but they will catch on when we are committed to being helpful to them.

I believe our job as parents is to make sure our little ones know that they know that they know we love them. Spend time and include them and make 'much' over them!

Learning

Children are never too young to learn and are happy to be included.

We all have things to share with others in our lives. As I mentioned, men and young men are great cooks, chefs, barbecue-ers, and bakers! Children love to learn and sometimes they know what questions to ask and sometimes they don't, but you can ask them and see how much they understand what you're trying to share with them.

Some of the different things we can cook or bake with our children are: cookies, pancakes, pies, cakes or cupcakes, pizza, bread in a bread machine is always fun, cornbread, fruit and cheese kabobs, smores, popcorn, pretzels, homemade ice cream, mac and cheese, hot dogs, hamburgers, chicken nuggets, any new recipe, and, if you are very brave, a fancy dinner.

So, get the kids together and, if they're old enough, enlist
them to chop the vegetables, and let the fun begin!

FUN
No
matter
what
you
choose

to
make…
whether
fun
kid
food…

desserts
or
chicken
or
beef
or
pasta….

or
vegetarian
or
really
fun food…
just
remember to
have fun!

10

Spring Fun

Spring Crafts and Activities

For most of my life, I lived in Ohio where we had four true seasons. The winters were brutal and Spring was a welcome time even with rain and up-and-down weather. The summers were quite warm and Fall was delightfully perfect. I can still remember how the leaves changed colors and the cooler wind blew gently to comfort us after the heat of Summer. Good times.

Now, however, I live where there is almost no discernable change in the seasons. To be honest, some joke our weather is 'hot' and 'hotter.' This is true. Winter is a paradise and we may see temperatures dip into the forties once in a while, however, the days recover to about 70 degrees usually. We enjoy a break from the sweltering heat of summer but, once you get acclimated to the heat, you barely notice it. I know it's difficult to believe, but it's true. I also understand there is a delay in Spring in Maine.

So, wherever you may be, I'm sure Spring is a great season! Let's get going!

Spring is the time for planting flowers and trees and small gardens; time to prepare the flower pots! So, get your little artists and their brushes and paints, and get them busy making the most beautiful pots you can imagine!

Growing seeds in a jar or eggshell may help get flowers or vegetables started.

There are many ways to make paper flowers.

Butterflies and cute little caterpillars are both great spring craft ideas. One of my personal favorites is pom-pom caterpillars and I also love thumbprint art.

Rainbows are easily made with colored paper or fruit loops or stained glass or pie plates and ribbon.

Spring is fun times. We filled our days with hikes, baking cookies shaped like flowers and spring things, and making pancakes like any other time of the year. We also did all sorts of crafts like wreaths of sunflowers with a soft message to children as well as ladybugs, umbrellas,

raindrop sun catchers, frogs made from paper plates, and many more fun spring crafts.

We also made bird feeders and filled them with seeds for our feathered friends. We hung hummingbird feeders after learning how to make sugar water to fill them with. I love those cute little birds and am always amazed when I see them. I understand they are the only birds that can maneuver backwards and they seem very skilled at this! Spring brings all the birds back to us as well as all the flowers.

Spring seems windier than summer, so I think it's a great season to fly kites. And, flying kites is a great family fun thing to do, it takes everyone to lovely spots to try to get that kite into the air, and only requires a few items to have a great time! So, pick a kite, head to a beach or field, and hope for wind!

Other Spring ideas include growing a garden with plants and bushes that attract butterflies or just a floral garden with beautiful seasonal flowers. In Ohio, some of the plants I loved to plant each spring did not survive the harsh winters there, however, they do survive all year in Florida! I love seeing my lantanas growing and flowering all year long where I live.

So, not only planting and having fun planting, are great activities for Spring, but learning about where you live and where others live can be educational as well.

I also try to keep a collection of coloring books for youngsters to enjoy when there seems to be nothing else to do. I also suggest cutting pictures from magazines and gluing them to cardboard to make a Spring collage.

Rainy Day Activities

Since Spring is a season notorious for rain – we always said April showers bring May flowers – we want to include some 'rainy day' fun ideas.

Dressing for the puddles helps as well as learning to make origami boats, animals, and many other things, karaoke, movies with popcorn, Legos, marble races, creating a time capsule, eating a meal together or having ice cream at a diner counter, going flea market or garage shopping, looking through a book of riddles to stimulate our brains, and more.

On rainy days, or any day, card games, board games, and more are great fun. Pictionary happens to be one of my favorite games because it promotes 'figuring out' skills as well as art skills. And, did I mention, it's fun and gets children off their phones and social media! My favorite thing to do. Children are only young for a short time and my 'soap box' is to not have them spend their precious childhood on their phones!

HOW TO PLAY PICTIONARY

The truth is, I'm no singer. I always say I have a voice only God can stand! Ha ha. But I think it's fun to sing even if you're not the best singer in the group. I believe children should be allowed to achieve their goals and, if they have a goal to be a singer, great, but if they just want to enjoy singing, even better. Everyone can enjoy things even if they don't pursue it as a career or dream job. And, did I mention, it's fun?

I'm sure karaoke machines range in price and quality, but any will do for the kids to have a great time.

A fun game of charades is another activity to consider with the neighborhood.

11

Summer Fun

Summer Crafts and Activities

Every year I and my friends and brothers looked forward to Summer. I love learning, but being free from school was a terrific time. Mom purchased passes for us at the local pool and I joined the swim team as well as we swam daily and had such a great time. I took a few swimming lessons and feel *every* child should learn to swim!

One of the other things I did over summer vacation was pick books to read. Since I could pick anything I wanted to read, I always picked something with horses. I loved them as a young girl and still love them today. Walter Farley's *Black Stallion* series was my favorite. I also loved little unknown books like, *A Horse Called Bonnie*. Whatever interest the children or adults in your life have, there's a book for everyone.

There are reading clubs and contests for the young ones to have fun joining.

In Ohio, summertime was also fair time! It was a great time for us because we raced harness horses at the different fairs and we made it a family thing too. When we went to the fair, we took the whole fair in – the rides, the food, the kids' crafts with melons and other produce, the sewing contests, pie eating contests, and more.

One of my favorite things about the fair is the children and their animals. Once I saw a young man cleaning the feet of his chicken with a toothbrush as the chicken stood perfectly still on a stump. And, in another area, some young girls were blow-drying their chickens they just bathed! The chickens had 'skinny eyes' as the hair dryer wind blew over them and their now beautifully white feathers fluffed.

If this gives you an idea for 4-H participation in your area, great! It's a great program to engage young people in farm life.

Another fun summer activity to try is to take a garden gnome everywhere you go, take pics and make a scrapbook. It's a fun project because it gets you and your children out of the house, enjoying exercise, seeing new places, away from cells and tells (short code for television), and can be saved for years to come to remember time spent together.

Journalling goes along with this as well. Journalling helps with writing skills, creative thought processes, and expression of feelings.

There are so many things to do in the warm weather. Water in any form is great. Whether there's a neighborhood pool close – or in your own backyard – or you live near a pond or spring like we do or the beach if you have one, cooling off in the water is wonderful.

Some spend time hiking along nature trails or canoeing and kayaking. It's nice to be out among nature if you are safe doing so.

As a young girl, my neighborhood friends and I played baseball, played board games, went for ice cream, enjoyed karaoke, built obstacle courses, and enjoyed various exercise activities and friendly competition.

Badminton or volleyball is great if you have others interested in these as well. We also gathered friends from the neighborhood and visited the local drive-in theater with soda and snacks. Movie theater movies were always on our to-do list as well.

Making homemade lemonade is also one of my very favorite things to do.

Inside and quiet activities include coloring books and projects to cut out pictures from magazines or draw art and glue them to a poster board to make a summer collage.

Pick berries

Attend an outdoor concert or play

Try new food

Watch a baseball game

Fishing and jumping rope are great.

Encourage Random Acts of Kindness.

Getting children started young at the barbecue is a fun summer activity as well as scavenger hunts, playing on the playground, visiting a farmer's market, or bowling.

One of my all-time favorite things to do is to be out in nature looking at different birds. While I love Osprey, once I saw an Eagle land on Daytona Beach. Someone suggested it may have been an Osprey. No way would I not know!

Visiting an Audubon Society can get you up close and personal with owls and other raptors as well.

If you don't have a local waterpark, a sprinkler will do. This, in addition to the ocean or spring swimming we talked about above.

There are so many things to do in the summer. A few more great ideas are making smores at an evening campfire and feeding ducks at a local neighborhood – in Florida we feed the turtles in the water as well! You can pretend to be a tourist in your own town. We do it all the time in Florida. Since it's the vaca-spot of America, we are inundated with tourists, so we act like them sometimes. We take pictures and pretend we are seeing things for the first time. Sometimes we look silly, but we have fun doing it. Growing vegetables and herbs or having a party in the evening with ice cream or freeze pops help cool everyone off.

And another really fun thing to do is hang out with your kids and teach them to play soccer or just balance the ball on your heads between each other. But, remember to have fun!

12

Fall/Harvest and Halloween Fun

Halloween is a FUN time for sure. My faith really doesn't allow me to celebrate this holiday, but I do for the children. I am not into 'ghosts' and 'goblins,' but my heart does not condemn me, so I see it as a fun thing and not anything bad. Forgive me if you disagree.

These fence posts painted as Dracula or Frankenstein or a cute ghost, can also be made on a smaller scale from popsicle sticks which confirms there are probably a million and one or more uses for popsicle sticks.

I hung ghosts in the trees at our home that were made of sheets wrapped around Styrofoam balls. I understand Halloween is the most decorated holiday second to Christmas. Many think it's super fun to dress up and have a good time collecting candy in the neighborhood.

I also liked to stuff pumpkin-colored garbage bags with leaves each fall and place them around the porch or the oak tree that grew in our front yard.

Apple bobbing or apple picking are great fall activities to do by oneself or with family. Since I don't have a family any longer, I still want to enjoy the season and enjoy making pies and apple sauce with my apples. Some cleverly know how to make apple chips as well with their apples. I also enjoy caramel-covered or candy-covered apples. Sometimes I bake the apples and add ice cream – YUM!

My Amish friends press the second apples – the ones that fell after we all picked the best apples – and make apple cider from these. I love this treat all year long, so I freeze it in small containers to enjoy all winter and into the next spring and summer!

chocolate covered strawberry "pumpkins"

PUMPKIN TREATS

PUMPKIN cupcakes

40+ Pumpkin Recipes for Babies and Kids

There are so many fun things to do with pumpkins - bread, soup, cupcakes....

...**Pumpkin** pie or pumpkin pie spice in a jar, pumpkin spice cinnamon rolls for breakfast – or anytime – pumpkin ice cream (yum), pancakes, pumpkin cider, pumpkin tea – if you can imagine that! – hand pies, cookies, candles, and more!

Each year, we hopped in the truck and headed for a local pumpkin patch. We enjoyed picking many pumpkins so we could host a pumpkin carving contest. One year over twenty children came to our harvest party. They all had carving tools and were given a pumpkin and went to work.

When I saw all the gorgeous pumpkins, it was impossible to pick a winner, but there was one young man who carved faces all around his pumpkin and each face was darling! I was so enamored with his work, I didn't realize how *much* I made over the little work of art, but it was unbelievably cute and clever. I always try to make *much* over all the children's pumpkins when we have a party.

Fall Crafts and Activities

Crafts, crafts, and more crafts! If you 'google' fall crafts, there will be so many projects, you will be very busy with paper pumpkins and wreaths, popsicle stick crafts, and much, much more!

Other things you may want to consider are creating or joining a scavenger hunt, arranging a fall bouquet, visiting a haunted house, making a tissue paper or finger-painted fall tree, having a not-so-scary movie night, a fashion show for costumes, dressing your dog or cat in a costume, take photos

family craft night
- themed -
Boo Basket

of your family, friends, home, fun activities you do this fall, enjoy a hayride, play in leaves, surprise a poor child with a boo-basket, build a haunted gingerbread house, have a bonfire or backyard fire, go on a fall hike, make popsicle stick scarecrows, make fall leaf lanterns or suncatchers, or find and color in coloring books special for fall activities.

There are fall games that you can enjoy. For instance, pumpkin and fun broom races, Halloween or fall time charades, Halloween or fall time bingo, Halloween or fall crossword puzzle, or word scramble, put the skeleton back together, pumpkin toss into containers, mummy bowling, pumpkin tic tac toe, and many, many more.

And, don't forget the snacks! You can pick from scary finger foods, hot dogs dressed like mummies with googly or mustard for eyes, ghost bananas, try out a Halloween Charcuterie Board, treats like rice crispy candy corn, eye cookies, and so much more for fall fun!

Thanksgiving Fun

Thanksgiving fun is part of fall fun to me. I enjoy the turkey crafts and looking forward to the parades and food – goodness - the food! Unbuckle those belts! I have never cooked a turkey myself, but I have eaten many. And, if you are a vegetarian, Tofurkey I believe is quite the Thanksgiving treat as well. And – the football – enough said.

Children can put together turkey snack bags,

Candy cornucopias

Turkey leaf lanterns

Turkey glove puppets

Hand and footprint turkeys

Or my favorite, a gratitude turkey using this pattern or construction paper feathers with things thankful for. There are so many things to do for Thanksgiving. Make every holiday one to remember!

13

Winter Fun

Winter Crafts and Activities

Winter is a different time for everyone. Growing up in Ohio, I thought everyone dealt with snow and cold and storms all winter and spent most of the winter indoors. Unless you were a skier, your options seemed limited.

I still enjoyed walks in the parks in the winter, but it was difficult to swing on swings comfortably in the cold weather. Temperatures could lower into the single digits or below zero at any time! It wasn't until I owned a horse who loved to ride in the snow that I really enjoyed the snow.

Now I live in Florida and Winter is the same as Spring, Summer, and Fall here. My brother used to say it was 'paradise' in the Winter. It is. We can kayak on the rivers and walk comfortably. The ocean is very cold, so when we see swimmers in the winter, we think they must be Canadians!! Ha ha.

In any event, there are some fun things to do if you are stuck indoors for your winter season.

I mentioned skiing – if your little one can ski like this one, you are going to want to get to the slopes.

The one and only time I skied I almost fell off the side of the mountain. So, I guess skiing is not something you pick up over a weekend as you attempt some quality family time.

Cross-country skiing has been a little more my speed and does provide great exercise. As long as you have snow, you don't necessarily need the hills.

Also, sledding is something I have enjoyed

along with indoor or outdoor ice skating

And, if you have a young hockey player in your family, winter is a great season for them. You can coach. Attending hockey games are also a great winter activity.

Also, snowmen of all sizes are fun to make if you live where snow is.

My favorite winter beverage is hot cocoa. There are so many variations of the treat and this size is just about right for me! Homemade is best and don't forget the marshmallows! You can host a hot cocoa party or a tea party on those cold days.

If you live where there is no snow – my mother always says our 'chance of snow today in central Florida is 0%' - ha has. I love that to be honest – then you have other options. Making snow is one option – some use soap bubbles to simulate snow and others have fun creating DIY snow globes!

Or making a winter wreath can be fun

Other ideas include writing someone. I'm sure there are friends and family everywhere that would love to receive a handwritten letter. When I first moved to Florida, I was lonely for home in Ohio. One connection I had was when my Amish friends wrote me and told me what they considered were all the mundane details of their lives. I missed all the ordinary life I had there and it was nice to see their letter and read and remember what life was like there.

Winter is the end of football season I believe. Probably a good time to plan a Super Bowl party and invite neighbors and friends or take a cooking class.

Even in Florida, it can get a little chilly, so anywhere we are can be a great place to whip up some homemade soup, chili, chicken pot pie, and more! I'm not the world's greatest cook so if I can make it, anyone can! Drag out those recipe books and find something warm and cozy to cook today! Homemade corn or other bread as toasted cheese or alone are best!

Since I love to create, I loved learning to

knit or crochet. Both are loads of fun and anyone can learn!

Other fun winter ideas include creating a gratitude journal. Thankfulness is a great thing to do any season of the year.

You can also have a family and friend photo shoot and keep the pictures in a photo album or scrapbook to keep great memories.

You can enjoy a spa day out or a warm bubbly bubble bath at home.

You can get all the clothing items or gloves or mittens you no longer wear and donate them to a homeless shelter or Goodwill.

You can find a winter coloring book or make a winter collage as well.

But no matter what you decide to do, make sure you have FUN!!

14

New Year's Fun

New Year's Crafts and Activities

New Year's is another great time to celebrate. You can make plans to stay in and invite others over for a fancy dinner party or have the children invite friends to a slumber party since the night usually extends to midnight and beyond!

It's always fun to learn about New Year's in other countries — for instance, it's called Omisoka in Japan.

One of my favorite things to do is have a pamper party — where the girls do nails and hair and may even apply temporary tattoos.

As always, you can make New Year's resolutions and create a thankful list for all you are thankful for in the past year. Some families like to have a slide show or, if they created a photo album for the fun they had the past year, take time to remember all the fun times. It allows everyone an opportunity to share their fun memories from the prior year.

Fun snacks for sure and you can consider popcorn balls with lots of different twists. Great yummy ideas are available.

If the Christmas tree is still up, it's fun to decorate it like a New Year's tree. One thing I try to do is decorate it with wishes and prayers. Anything you choose would be fun.

Countdown balloons are fun to make. You can put activity paper in each balloon for each hour with fun things to do. New Year's Eve Bingo is another great game idea for your New Year's celebration. And, don't forget to whip out the karaoke and sing everyone's fave – Auld Lang Syne. Many towns have fireworks as well.

One New Year's many years ago, a dear friend taught me a new tradition. He was a paralyzed veteran and I visited him on New Year's Eve. At midnight, he had me go to the kitchen, retrieve a metal pot, and hit it over and over. We laughed and I will never forget it.

15

Valentine Fun

Valentine Crafts and Activities

There could be an entire book devoted to fun for Valentine's Day. I will touch on a few of my faves and you can explore many more.

It's all about love and hearts of all kinds for Valentines. You can make candles like here, watercolor valentines, wreaths made from cut-out construction paper hearts, garlands made of hearts, or even hearts as suncatchers made with tissue paper over heart-shaped plastic templates as shown here.

If you're brave, you can try your

hand at melting crayons to make lovely hearts or little heart pillows like these shown here.

There are many crafts to choose from and kits available to everyone having a great time on Valentine's Day!

Clay hearts made from cookie cutters and or hand shaped are lovely.

Read Valentine's books.

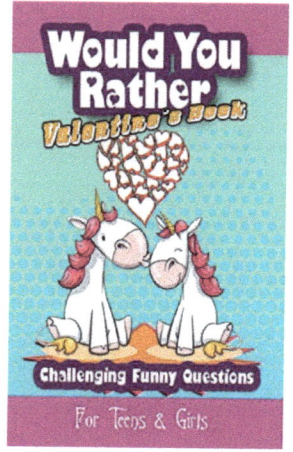

Write a poem or share Valentine facts about this special day.

Baking is a great holiday tradition — cookies, cupcakes, pastry, heart-shaped cherry hand pies, and more......

...and don't forget the chocolate suckers, lollipops, candy molds for chocolate hearts and more!

96

16

Mother's Day Fun

Mother's Day Crafts and Activities

Mother's Day is special to many. I have been blessed to be able to share Mother's Day with my mother for many, many years. I realize some don't have a perfect situation, so we apologize for a sensitive subject but hope all can be thankful for a mother in their lives. I consider myself a mother to my animals since I don't have children.

I understand the most sold flowers happens on Mother's Day. I love flowers myself and enjoy their beauty many days, not just holidays.

So, there are tons of crafts moms like to receive to cherish through the years. This is one example of something cute to let Mom know how much you love and appreciate her.

Some other ideas include treating her to a spa day either at home or at the spa. I personally love to have my nails done – especially my toenails.

Making mom a special meal or treating her to her favorite restaurant are other ideas for her special day. Just giving Mom a day off is a nice treat.

As I mentioned above, flowers are always nice. You can either buy them at the store, but if money is a little tight, like it is sometimes, you can always go to where wildflowers grow and pick her a huge bouquet of beautiful flowers and put them in a vase for her. Even if that vase is a make-shift one.

Homemade presents and homemade cards are the sweetest way to say, 'I love you' in my option.

A Mother's Day basket filled with her favorite things is always nice. Some moms like special treats they don't have all year.

Also, creating or picking a special song or video at home or church that tells her how much you love her or creating a 'chore' book listing the chores you promise to help with for her. A collage of the family or pictures in special lockets are nice gifts to make for Mom.

On Mother's Day, I purchased bricks for my mother. She loved them and they will forever be a testament to our being here, especially to remember the ones we've lost.

And I can't forget one of my favorites – dessert! There's always a reason to bake!

Happy Mother's Day!

17

Father's Day Fun

Father's Day Crafts and Activities

Father's Day is a way to thank Dad for everything he does for the family. I lost my dad several years ago and Father's Day has come to be a little sad, but I try to remember how much I loved him and I celebrate in a smaller way now, but I still honor him on this day. Again, some days are more difficult for families. I understand.

Our 'hats off' to dads! They are something very special and never seem to get the recognition they deserve, but their families always know how special they are. Where would the little ones be without them?

They sure do know how to go the extra miles. Especially when one of their little darlings invite them to tea!

You can't help but love them, that's for sure!

I admit it can be a challenge to decide exactly what wonderful thing to do for dad, some like a little pampering....

... but some just want time to read that paper!!! It's nice to spend time with Dad.

Some really love those thoughtful gifts that say so much....

But, to be honest, I think the generations of men would just love a great barbecue!

18

Labor Day-Memorial Day-July 4th Fun

Labor Day and Memorial Day and July 4th holidays are special to me. Always having been American and old enough to remember what brave men did to secure my freedom and the ability to enjoy the life I have, makes me truly grateful. I want to remember them and my country always. And also, the labor force that has made America great.

Some things I consider to celebrate these days are to have a moment of silence to remember those I know and those I did not know. I enjoy donating to veteran organizations and becoming aware of events and needs that local veterans may have.

I also decorate my home with flags and follow all the laws while doing so to honor my country the best way I know how.

Since these are National holidays, I usually have the time off and can plan a family outing or get together with friends.

Everyone loves fireworks. My brother-in-law was a paralyzed veteran and he could never get enough fireworks. He endured the loud sounds to enjoy watching the light show in the sky.

When I was a young girl, our residential block had a Labor Day parade every year. We were the only block in the neighborhood to do so. We decorated our bikes with red, white, and blue streamers and crepe paper and rode along with a fire truck and everyone else. It was a great time to celebrate.

For the 4th of July and Memorial Day, we had small twizzler-type sticks that sparkled after being lit. We all thought these were great when we were younger.

Concerts with patriotic music or television specials celebrating our country are always a fun idea for these holidays.

You may enjoy taking a virtual tour of the White House and another idea is to include a history lesson. A lesson about each of the holidays and the reason we celebrate them helps us appreciate our great country.

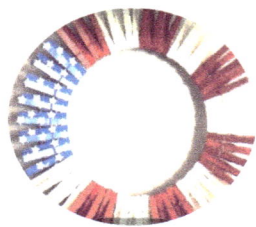

 Watching a patriotic movie may be a great activity for these holidays as well as there are terrific crafts for kids :

And, don't forget the Patriotic treats - cupcakes, cookies, and ice cream treats that are red, white, and blue.

102

19

Other Ideas

There are so many fun things to do. I hope I have not exhausted everyone with my Type-A personality. I'm all about getting as much life in as possible. My late brother lived life to the fullest. The thing I loved most about him was how every time we did the same thing, he was so excited and enjoyed it as if it was the first time we ever did whatever we were doing. Whether it was hiking or kayaking or going to the Florida Keys, he faced life with the joy of a child and the courage of a giant!! I hope everyone finds their way to doing this every day.

I admit I am adamantly opposed to children and adults being glued to social media or their phones. There is a great big and wonderful world all around us to see and experience in reality and I think we are missing too much to just sit at home and dream about doing something fun.

I've included some additional things and things that may be listed above but were worth mentioning again that I find fun and have enjoyed doing with friends, by myself, or with my stepdaughter and her friends.

Movie night – I've had movie night by myself or others. I would finish all my chores, make a snack or meal, settle all the pets, and hunker down in front of the television for one of my favorite movies or a new movie.

My father and I spent evenings watching a movie and eating fattening snacks. I treasure these special memories because they are some of the last memories I have of spending time with my father before he went to heaven.

I've also had a movie night with friends. One friend and I would put our families to bed and then sneak out together to make the late showing of a new flick. Sometimes we invited the children. When we did, there were many and we all squeezed into my small car and headed for the show. It looked like one of those 'clown cars' we hear about where many grown men get out of a tiny car! Afterward, my friend, the girls, and I enjoyed a snack and girl time at a local pie shop. Great memories. I allowed the girls to pick only *family* movies and we all enjoyed the time together.

Party night - Just a fun night with maybe pizza and pop and desserts. We hosted a 'fun' night at our house, played games, had food and desserts, and lots of fun.

Nature scavenger hunt – I hid candy and prizes for my girlfriend's two boys to find. They were so cute as they eagerly looked for the surprises and especially when they found them too. We did this outside at my 30-acre farm.

Puzzles – My sister and I can sit for hours doing puzzles. I think they help with many mental skills - like matching shapes and colors. It's not always an easy task to put them together. Puzzles were one way I had to get my father out of his bedroom he held up in and into the dining room. He shared memories of his mother putting puzzles together as well. We were able to talk, spend time together, and do something we could cherish forever because after finishing the puzzles, I glued them and framed some of them. I saved them all.

Make mailboxes - So you can write each other letters. This is a great way to improve writing skills. Mailboxes can be purchased – I guess they can be finished, but some craft stores or online stores have ones to decorate ourselves. I have seen these on sale at JoAnne's and other craft stores.

Write a children's book together or write a song together – Since I love children's literature, what better way to encourage verbalizing feelings or stories, creative writing, learning new words, putting words together, and making a story flow, than to create a little children's book? The young one may even be able to do the art-work for the book as well. Children are very creative and curiosity is something that allows them to create new stories. If they need information on a certain subject, it allows the adult and child to 'google' information and learn with the child too.

Books – Children's books for young – like chapter books. The classics with teens are a great bonding and quality time spent together activity. Reading is a struggle for me since I have dyslexia. This no longer hinders me since I learned that Mozart's music fixes dyslexia and it did for me! Listening to the Sonata for Two Pianos and the Violin Concertos – especially 2, 3, and 4 – have helped to heal the mixed-up connections in my brain that have led to jumbling numbers and words as I try to read them. This has helped me a great deal to enjoy more reading. When I was still struggling to read, I would pick a book for me and my stepdaughter to read and I read a chapter when she was at school and then, when she came home, she read the chapter and then we talked about it. Not only was this a great way to spend time with her, she learned to read, remember what she read, and tell someone (me) about what she read.

I think reading many different things allows a child to enjoy life. I never read *Moby Dick* and others and wish I had. The other classics like Robinson Caruso, ... and more are interesting and I think children should be encouraged to read.

Create a memory book – I mentioned this already, but taking pictures of times spent – nature hikes, museums, art events, fun times, parties, and celebrations the family has done – can be great ways to enjoy memories. There is a story for every picture. This encourages photography, writing and reading skills, and helps the young brain be happy. It is really good for a person's brain to have memories that make the them happy.

Miniature golf – Who doesn't like a round of miniature golf? I am no golfer, to say the least. Hitting balls for great distances and walking or golf cart riding around to find them and hit them again does not appeal to me – but it does to some – but anyone can enjoy miniature golf.

Model airplane or boat – I love this little picture because you can make cute things with any age child, however, with older children this is also a great project. These are great projects for men to do with sons. Sometimes it seems moms do most things, but dads can be involved as well. Putting models together is a special talent. Drones, if allowed in your area, are fun to operate as well.

I've seen boats that are made to put into water and remotely sail around. Looks like a ton of fun. The model airplanes and helicopters look a little more complicated and adult supervision is recommended for any of these projects for sure.

Magic tricks – Learning magic can be really fun to do for friends and family. There are some easy tricks and, depending on the age of the child – or adult, – tricks can be simple or more complex.

Berry picking – You can make a pie or jelly or just eat the great fruit. One of my favorite things to do is to go berry picking. Many places allow picking blueberries, raspberries, mulberries, strawberries, and more.

I also want to include apples and pears here because I lived near an apple orchard in Ohio where I could pick those as well. Pears can be used to make pies just like apples and they are delicious.

Not only are these nutritional snacks, you can also spend time with your child baking that pie and enjoy eating it with them and the family.

Have a NO TV or NO PHONES night – This sounds so simple, but sometimes it's a real challenge. It's difficult to believe our ancestors did not have phones or television. How *did* they manage?

When the electricity goes off during a storm is when I realize how difficult it has become to have a real conversation with family. This had not ought be! We fumble around for a book to read or a game to play, but what about just talking or playing a game to allow conversation? My brother and I break out the Yahtzee!

Games like 'I Spy' or counting cars if you take a drive, or remembering all the fun things you did one year ago can be another way to make a new memory together.

Go to a play – Or you can be in a play or put one on. When I was young, my girlfriends and I would act out certain plays. We only knew stories like Cinderella, however, you can take a favorite children's book and put on a play yourself, or you can go to the nearby theater or school having a play and watch a play.

Try new food – I think it's fun to try something new. There are Thai restaurants, Hungarian restaurants, and more. Once I took shrimp to my Amish friends and their reaction was astounding to me. They didn't know what it was and didn't even want to try it as I showed them how delicious the shrimp were to eat.

I see different and new food items at the grocery store every day. I don't usually buy processed food, but some food looks fun – like new dumplings or pizza rolls. I sometimes hear of new ways to enjoy pizza. Try something you have never tried before. It may become your new favorite!

Tea party – Perhaps for small children a 'hot chocolate' party would be better than a tea party – but for adults who enjoy sharing time together or older children who enjoy different flavors of tea, any beverage will do with a light snack and some witty banter between everyone. Hospitality!

Plant a tree or flowers – A garden with vegetables and caring for them is a great thing to do with children. Planting beautiful flowers teaches children to appreciate nature. Talking about bees and butterflies while doing this as well as how planting trees helps the environment and the world fosters learning. A vegetable garden is great for

106

growing beets, carrots, potatoes, tomatoes, cucumbers, squash, pumpkins, and more.

Play frisbee – This is a great game to play to get some exercise and develop coordination skills as well. Any park or backyard will do and frisbees are generally not very expensive.

Watch the sunrise or sunset – My mom loves to watch the sunrise and the sunset. When we vacationed at the panhandle of Florida, we would get up every morning and rush to the east side of the cabin where the Gulf of Mexico would welcome the rising sun. The start of a brand-new day. What would we do today?

Then, each evening, after we had fun, swam, talked, ate, rested, and more, we would rush to the west side of the cabin where the Atlantic Ocean would send the sun down over the horizon to conclude another wonderful day of great memories.

It was a time we reflected on the day, sometimes made plans for the next day, or just simply watched as the daylight ended; sending us to our cabins to finish out the rest of the evening rituals and then to bed!

Camping –At a campground or in the backyard. Camping is a great family activity, but if you don't have a camper or tent and the campground doesn't rent cabins where you want to go, you can still make a tent from blankets in your backyard and have blankets or sleeping bags to sleep in if you are in a safe place - and there are no poisonous snakes, bear, or other things that go bump in the night! In Ohio, we didn't have much to worry about - a stray raccoon or possum here and there, but in Florida, many dangerous things can come around in the dark.

So, some places require the safety of a camper or cabin. Be safe and know.

Study the stars – There's a program for electronic devices that, if you point your device to the stars, it tells you the constellations. My brother-in-law introduced me to

this and it was remarkable to me because I couldn't distinguish the Milky Way from the Little Dipper to be honest. But, suddenly, even I appeared to be a genius identifying Orion and other stars in the sky.

Also, the world is a big place but, with a globe, it seems a little smaller and we all seem a little closer together. It's more fun to learn when we are with those we love. Every moment is memorable with family doing what makes us happy.

School projects – Helping and monitoring homework and course studies allows children to know they are alright. This was another great way to spend quality time with my stepdaughter. One year she had a project – I was tempted to say *we* had a project because I am ever *too* involved – where she was asked to collect different types of seeds, mount them on a board, and put the names of the seeds on the board.

We collected over fifty different types of seeds and had a great time collecting them, gluing them to the board, and she wrote what they are called on the board. She was so proud to take her board to school to show her teacher all she collected and learned about.

This can be done with any project – whether it's doing shadowbox creations for stories or lessons children are being taught or even writing a review of a movie or book or newspaper or magazine article.

These activities allow the parent to judge how well the child understands the school information they are learning and to help where needed. I have to watch that I don't *complete* the whole project at times because I'm such the overachiever and this doesn't allow for growth and learning by the child.

Any outside activity–is a good activity. Whether you are investigating rocks, trees, animals, birds, and more, getting out and enjoying nature as well as learning something is always good for a child and even adults.

I live where there are too many plants and trees to name. I could probably spend a year trying to figure out all the different types of palm trees that grow in Florida.

Outdoor activities promote interest in the world around children and adults. It also helps children and adults look for things to learn about and enjoy in the world around them. They ask questions and get answers when they wonder what type of rock is at the beach – coquina rocks are sedentary rocks found at the ocean and are a rare form of limestone composed of collections of shell fragments from mollusks. So, there's a lesson on what's special about coquina – soft in the water – hardens when in the air and is used for building… and what's a mollusk – clams, snails, slugs, squids – gastropods, bivalves, cephalopods, scaphopods…. GOOGLE has all the info!

Incubate a chicken or raise chicks – there's a little miracle happening inside that little egg! When the egg is fertilized, a chick grows around it and when it's time to come out of that shell, it makes its own little hole and you can hear it cheep-cheep-cheeping! When they get themselves out of that egg, it is amazing to watch those

cute little things run around on tiny little legs and keep cheeping!

Visit a farm – If you live in the city, visit a farm to see another way of life and see farm animals.

Visit a city – If you live on a farm, visit a city to see another way of life and how city folk live.

Bike rides - Are always good exercise at any age. I've been able to increase the distance I can ride and ride the same distance faster. There are even great – sometimes a little expensive – electric bikes for ways to have fun at any age!

Marital Arts – My brother enjoyed learning a martial art – Taekwondo – to be specific. He advanced to black belt and was so proud of this achievement. All children want to know is that you're proud of them. It means so much to them. No matter what they choose to do or how old they are.

Have a fun night out - My stepdaughter and I had many fun nights out. One such night is when we dressed up and went to a local ice cream parlor with a carousel in the center of the store. The carousel rotated just like a real carousel. We loved to sit on the rotating carousel, order our ice cream, look over the other treats in the store, enjoy our ice cream, and then head home.

On other nights, we invited all her friends over and had waffle bowls and waffle cones, several different flavors of ice cream, toppings of all sorts, and whipping cream for each friend to make their own ice cream treats.

Make every moment a moment together – We always made my stepdaughter part of our lives. She went everywhere with us and there was no place she wasn't happy to be. It was fun growing up again with her. One childhood didn't seem enough for me.

There are so many fun things to do…

……make life extraordinary!!! In every way….

teach
them
what
you
know

and let them explore and enjoy…….. and make

sure
all
have
FUN
FUN
FUN!

..... and